Perfectly
· Simple ·

Pasta

Marilyn Bright

ILLUSTRATED BY CARL MELEGARI

Appletree Press

First published in 1992 by
The Appletree Press Ltd,
7 James Street South, Belfast BT2 8DL.

Perfectly Simple: Pasta

A note on measures

Imperial, metric and American measures have
been given for all recipes, which are for four
people unless otherwise stated.

A catalogue record for this book is
available from the British Library.

ISBN 0-86281-332-8

9 8 7 6 5 4 3 2 1

Introduction

Did Italian explorers discover pasta in China, or did Marco Polo merely report finding Chinese pasta "like ours"? The controversy continues, but the glories of fresh pasta have been rediscovered and have spread far beyond the shores of Italy and China. Recent dietary trends towards higher fibre and carbohydrate intake have rehabilitated pasta with a positive health image. New generations of cooks have turned to fresh home-made pastas and added their own variations to old traditions.

Fresh vegetables, meat and fish team up with inventive sauces; old recipes are given twentieth-century updating with ingredients that might have startled Mrs Beeton. At the same time, combinations such as pasta, tomatoes and cheese never lose their charm, simply because they taste so nice together.

Being agreeably inexpensive in itself, good pasta deserves the best of accompaniments – good olive oil, fresh herbs and, most importantly, good cheese. Take a vow to avoid the pre-grated stuff and treat yourself to the joys of fine cheese freshly grated over hot pasta. With a little butter and freshly-milled black pepper, such simple fare is the food of kings.

Most of the recipes in this little book are quite flexible, and types of pastas indicated are often interchangeable, according to the cook's fancy. Unless otherwise indicated, *al dente* cooking of pasta is preferred, that is, pasta cooked not totally soft, but with some resistance "to the tooth".

Béchamel Sauce

Delicately-flavoured white sauce, or *béchamel*, is used in many of the baked pasta dishes and is the versatile base for a classic cheese sauce.

2oz/50g/4 tbsp butter
1 pt/570ml/2 cups milk
2oz/50g/^{1}/$_3$ cup flour
salt
freshly-grated nutmeg

Melt butter over low heat, stir in flour and cook for a minute. Gradually add milk and continue to stir over heat until mixture is smooth and thickened. Season to taste with salt and nutmeg. If sauce is not to be used immediately, cover surface with a greaseproof buttered paper to prevent skin from forming.

Cheese Sauce

Stir 4oz/110g/1 cup grated cheese into the thickened *béchamel* sauce while it is still hot. A pinch of mustard powder may be added if liked.

Sauce Napoli

Fresh-flavoured tomato sauce and pasta is a gastronomic partnership that has survived the test of time, travelling from the Mediterranean to nearly every corner of the globe. Unless you have a source of home-grown sun-ripened tomatoes, the tinned Italian sort are the best to use.

2 tbsp/30ml olive oil
2 cloves garlic, finely chopped
1 tsp/5ml sugar
2 tsp/10ml dried oregano
fresh basil leaves to garnish (optional)
1 onion, finely chopped
2 x 14oz/396g tins chopped tomatoes
2 tbsp/30ml tomato purée
salt, freshly ground black pepper

Heat the oil and gently sauté the onion and garlic until soft. Add the remaining ingredients, cover and cook for 20–30 minutes or until sauce is slightly thickened. Serve over hot pasta with fresh basil leaves strewn over.

Bolognese Sauce

Known as *ragu* in its native Italy, this rich, meaty sauce is a classic feature with spaghetti, or layered between tender leaves of baked lasagna.

3 tbsp/45ml olive oil
1 onion, finely chopped
1 carrot, finely chopped
1 clove garlic, finely chopped
1 stick of celery, finely chopped
3oz/80g streaky bacon, finely chopped
8oz/225g lean minced beef
4 fl oz/110ml/$^1/_2$ cup red wine
14oz/396ml tin of tomatoes
8 fl oz/225ml/1 cup stock
1 tbsp/30ml tomato purée
freshly-grated nutmeg
salt and freshly-ground black pepper

Heat the oil and gently cook the onion, carrot, garlic and celery until softened. Add the bacon and the minced beef and stir over heat until evenly browned. Add wine, tomatoes, stock, purée and a little grating of nutmeg. Cover the pan and simmer gently for 30–40 minutes, adding a little water if mixture starts to stick. Taste and add salt if needed, and black pepper.

Fresh Egg Pasta

Home-made pasta is a special gourmet treat, with greater flavour than the store-bought variety. In addition to cooking in a quarter of the time, it opens new possibilities for the cook's creativity with fillings and artistic shapes. Strong flour of the sort used for bread making is recommended for hand-rolled pasta.

1 lb/450g/4 cups flour
4 large eggs
1 tsp salt
6–7 tbsp/90–105ml water

Sift flour and salt into a large bowl and make a well in the centre. Break eggs into the well and gradually stir the flour and eggs together, adding water in small amounts as necessary to make a soft dough. Form dough into a ball and knead on a floured surface until it feels firm and elastic, about 10 minutes.

Divide dough into two or more pieces and, on a floured surface, roll each out as thin as possible. The grain of a wooden table should be visible through it. Leave rolled sheets to dry for 30 minutes, then roll up into a scroll and cut into strips of the width desired, or into other shapes. Spread cut pasta on a cloth or on improvised racks to dry until needed for cooking.

Maccheroni alla Carbonara

Delicious "charcoal-makers" pasta is the perfect quick meal, using ingredients most likely to be at hand. Romans, who claim invention of this dish, most often use macaroni or thick-ribbed rigatoni, but Spaghetti Carbonara has become an international favourite.

4oz/110g ham or bacon
1 tbsp/15ml butter
14oz/400g macaroni or spaghetti
2 large eggs, beaten
3oz/80g/$^2/_3$ cup grated Parmesan cheese
freshly-ground black pepper

Cut the ham or bacon into matchsticks and fry in the butter. Cook macaroni in plenty of boiling salted water; drain, and put into a heated dish. Quickly stir the eggs into the cooked bacon and pour the mixture over the hot pasta. When all is well mixed, stir in the Parmesan cheese, reserving some to serve separately. Season well with black pepper and serve hot.

Pasta Baked with Mushrooms

Dried ceps, *trompettes-des-maures*, or your favourite wild mushrooms add special flavour to this vegetarian main-course dish. It can be assembled in advance, ready to slide into the oven when needed.

1oz/25g dried wild mushrooms
1oz/25g/2 tbsp butter
4oz/100g fresh mushrooms, sliced
4 spring onions, finely chopped
³/4pt/425ml/1¹/2 cups béchamel sauce
12oz/350g/approx. 3 cups any pasta shapes
salt, pepper
2oz/50g/¹/2 cup grated cheese
finely chopped parsley to garnish

Soak the dried mushrooms in hot water until soft, then drain and chop coarsely. Melt butter and cook fresh mushrooms until soft, then stir in spring onions and soaked dried mushrooms and cook for a further minute. Remove from heat and stir in *béchamel* sauce. Cook pasta shapes in boiling salted water until just slightly underdone. Drain and combine with mushroom sauce. Season to taste with salt and pepper, then turn into greased baking dish and sprinkle cheese on top. Bake in oven pre-heated to gas mark 4, 350°F, 180°C for about 30 minutes, or until pasta is heated through and top is golden brown. Serve garnished with chopped parsley.

Pasta Primavera

Tender young vegetables lend springtime colour to pale green pasta ribbons in a simple wine and cream sauce. The vegetables can be varied according to what is in season.

2 carrots
4 spring onions, shredded lengthwise
6oz/170g fresh asparagus
3oz/80g mangetout
4 tbsp/60ml dry white wine
8 fl oz/225ml/1 cup cream
12oz/325g green fettucine or tagliatelle
salt, pepper

Cut carrots into thin matchsticks. Cut shredded onions and asparagus into similar lengths. Blanch vegetables in a small amount of boiling water 2–3 minutes or until just *al dente*. Drain and set aside. Put wine into a saucepan and quickly reduce by half. Reduce heat and pour in cream to thicken gently while pasta is cooking in boiling, salted water. When pasta is nearly cooked, stir blanched vegetables into cream sauce to heat through. Season with salt and pepper and pour over drained cooked pasta.

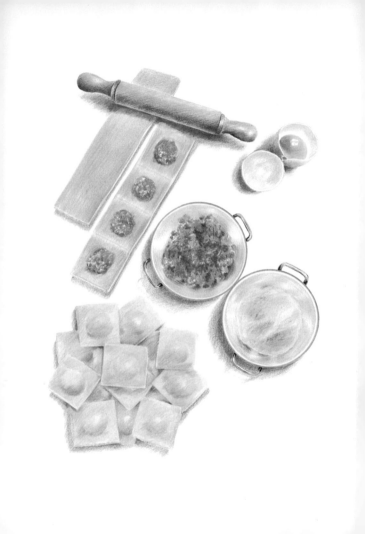

Tortelli Stuffed with Spinach and Cheese

These delicious stuffed cushions of pasta are not beyond the abilities of novice cooks and well worth the time involved. Tortelli can be made early in the day, ready to be heated with butter and cheese, or baked in sauce when needed.

🍴

1 batch fresh egg pasta (p.11)
Filling:
4oz/110g/¹/₂ cup cooked spinach, drained and puréed
4oz/110g/¹/₂ cup cream cheese
4 tbsp/60ml grated Parmesan cheese
1 egg, beaten
salt, pepper
freshly-grated nutmeg

Squeeze as much liquid as possible from the spinach, then combine with the cream cheese, Parmesan cheese and enough beaten egg to make a soft paste. Season with salt, pepper and grated nutmeg. Roll pasta into two rectangles, slightly thicker than for tagliatelle. Working quickly, lightly mark one of the rectangles into 2-inch squares. Place a teaspoonful of filling in each square. Use water or the leftover beaten egg to moisten along the scored lines with a pastry brush. Place remaining pasta sheet on top and press along cutting lines to seal well. Cut into squares and press edges again. Cook tortelli in boiling salted water, a few at a time, until they rise to the top, about 4–5 minutes. Serve hot with melted butter and grated cheese or baked in the oven in tomato sauce.

Pasta with Smoked Salmon and Dill Cream

Pale pink ribbons of salmon and green-flecked sauce inspire the cook to be art director. Choose butterfly or bow shapes, nests of fine-spun vermicelli, or tagliatelle in natural or green tints.

🐝

1 lb/450g pasta shapes
6 fl oz/170ml/³/4 cup double cream
3oz/80g cream cheese
2 tsp lemon juice
1 tsp anchovy paste or dill sprigs to garnish
freshly-ground black pepper
6oz/170g smoked salmon, thinly sliced
2 tbsp fresh chopped dill,
2 tsp dried dill weed

Put pasta on to cook according to directions. Make sauce by gently heating cream with cream cheese, beating until smooth. Season with lemon juice, anchovy paste and freshly-ground black pepper. Cut smoked salmon into ¹/2 in ribbons and stir into the sauce with the chopped dill. Drain pasta, stir in sauce and transfer to heated dish. Garnish with dill sprigs.

Macaroni Vegetable Pie

Classic macaroni cheese becomes a party centrepiece in this vegetable-sparked version, which is topped with a golden-brown lattice of pastry.

8oz/225g macaroni
1 tbsp olive oil
1 medium courgette, sliced
1 onion, finely chopped
1 small red pepper, diced
4oz/110g/1 cup tinned corn kernels
1 clove garlic
³/₄ pt/425g/1¹/₂ cups cheese sauce (p.4)
3 tbsp parsley, chopped
6 oz/170g puff pastry
1 small egg, beaten

Cook the macaroni in boiling salted water until slightly underdone. Drain and set aside. Heat olive oil in a pan and stir-fry the courgette, onion, pepper, corn and garlic until onion is slightly softened. In a large bowl, combine the cooked macaroni, vegetables, cheese sauce and parsley. Turn mixture into a greased ovenproof dish. Roll out puff pastry and cut into ¹/₂ in / 1.5 cm strips. Lay pastry strips over mixture to form a lattice pattern and brush with beaten egg. Bake in oven pre-heated to gas mark 4, 350°F, 180°C until pastry is golden brown and pie is heated through, about 25 minutes.

Seafood Stuffed Pasta Shells

Large pasta shells filled with seafood make an eye-catching starter or main course for entertaining. The recipe is adaptable for fresh or tinned fish according to the season.

12 extra-large pasta shells
1 tbsp butter
3oz/85g mushrooms, finely chopped
4 spring onions, finely chopped
12oz/340g/2 cups flaked, cooked salmon, crab or tuna
8–10 black olives, finely chopped
3 tbsp/45ml parsley, finely chopped
3oz/85g cream cheese
lemon juice
salt, pepper
1 egg yolk
³/₄ pt/425ml/1¹/₂ cups béchamel sauce (p.4)

Cook pasta shells according to directions, drain and set aside. Heat butter and sauté the chopped mushrooms and onions until soft. Remove from heat and combine with the flaked fish, olives, parsley and cream cheese. Season to taste with lemon juice, salt and pepper. Stir in egg yolk and carefully spoon mixture into cooked shells. Arrange in greased ovenproof dish and spoon sauce over. Bake in oven pre-heated to gas mark 4, 350°F, 180°C until shells are heated through.

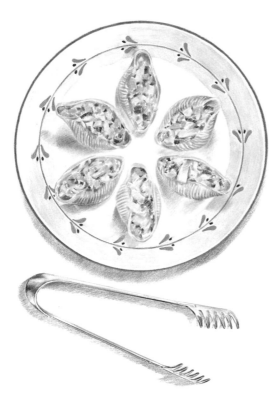

Ham and Leek Baked Lasagna

Pre-cooked lasagna leaves have made easy work of layered pasta dishes. This creamy ham-and-leek version can be assembled a day ahead and refrigerated until needed.

❦

8oz/225g cooked smoked ham, thickly sliced
2 tbsp butter
1 lb/450g/5 cups sliced leeks
1 1/2pt/850ml/3 3/4 cups béchamel sauce (p.4)
8oz/225g/2 cups grated mature cheddar
8oz/225g lasagna leaves, pre-cooked type

Cut ham slices into 1/2 in squares. Heat butter in a large pan and gently cook ham pieces with leeks until slightly softened. In a greased ovenproof dish, alternate layers of sauce, leek mixture, grated cheese and pasta leaves until ingredients are used up. Finish with a cheese layer. Bake in oven pre-heated to gas mark 5, 375°F, 190°C for about 30 minutes, until golden brown on top.

Five-Pepper Pasta

The heat in this south-of-the-border sauce is determined by the type and quantity of chilli peppers used. Tiny red ones are usually the most incendiary, with pale green ones at the milder end of the heat spectrum.

1 red pepper
1 yellow pepper
1 green pepper
4 tbsp/60ml/¹/₄ cup olive oil
3 tbsp/45ml tomato purée
1 ripe tomato, peeled, de-seeded and chopped
1–4 chilli peppers, de-seeded and chopped
1 clove garlic
lemon juice
salt
1 lb/450g rigatoni
freshly-grated Parmesan cheese
coarsely-cracked black peppercorns

Grill the red, yellow and green peppers, turning frequently until the skin is blistered and charred. Rub off the skin and rinse, then de-seed and cut peppers into strips. Put half the red pepper into a blender with the olive oil, tomato purée, chopped tomato, chilli peppers and garlic, and process to make sauce. Season to taste with lemon juice and salt. Cook rigatoni according to directions, drain and stir in pepper strips and sauce. Serve with Parmesan cheese and cracked peppercorns sprinkled over.

Tuoni e Lampo

"Thunder and lightning" in English, this frugal Italian dish was traditionally made from the broken pasta at the bottom of the sack. This recipe uses chick peas but lentils, pinto beans and other pulses make equally successful combinations.

8oz/225g dried chick peas
2 tbsp/30ml olive oil
1 onion, chopped
1 clove garlic, crushed
sprig of fresh thyme
12oz/350g/approx. 3^1/$_2$ cups broken pasta or
pasta shapes
sauce napoli (p.7)
freshly-grated Parmesan cheese

Soak chick peas overnight. Next day, heat olive oil in a large pan and sauté the onion and garlic until soft. Add chick peas and thyme and cover with water to a depth of 1 in / 3 cm. Cook for 3–4 hours or until chick peas are tender and have absorbed most of their cooking liquid. Meanwhile, cook pasta, drain and combine with hot chickpeas, adding salt to taste. Serve with Sauce Napoli and Parmesan cheese.

Vermicelli with Artichoke Hearts

Fine "angel hair" pasta makes an elegant starter or summer dish when swirled into nests with marinated artichoke hearts and dotted with toasted pine nuts. Substitute almond slivers if pine nuts are difficult to find.

4 fl oz/110ml/^{1}/$_2$ cup olive oil
2 tbsp white wine vinegar
2 tbsp/30ml lemon juice
1 clove garlic, crushed
1 small chilli pepper, split
salt
14oz/396g tin artichoke hearts, drained
12oz/340g vermicelli
1oz/25g/3 tbsp toasted pine nuts

Combine olive oil, vinegar, lemon juice, garlic and chilli pepper in a small saucepan. Season with salt and heat gently without allowing to come to boil. Remove garlic and chilli pepper and pour hot marinade over artichoke hearts. Set aside to cool. Cook vermicelli according to directions, taking care not to overcook. Drain pasta and toss in some of the marinade from artichokes. Swirl into nests on 4 serving plates, place artichoke hearts in centre and sprinkle with pine nuts. Drizzle over a little more marinade and serve.

Spaghetti alle Vongole

Vongole are small clams which feature in this pasta favourite from the south of Italy. Other shellfish can be used, singly or in whatever mixture might appeal. Fresh mussels in their shiny black shells look particularly attractive.

3–4 lb/1.5–2 kg fresh clams in shells
3 tbsp/45ml olive oil
1 small onion, finely chopped
2 cloves garlic, finely chopped
14oz/396g tin chopped tomatoes
8 tbsp/¹⁄₂ cup finely chopped parsley
14oz/400g spaghetti

Scrub shellfish and rinse under running water to remove grit. Steam in a closed pan over hot water until shells open; discard any that remain closed. Heat oil and gently sauté onion and garlic until softened, then stir in tomatoes and cook until sauce is slightly thickened. Stir in opened shellfish and chopped parsley and pour over spaghetti which has been cooked *al dente*.

Classic Cannelloni

Creamy tubes of pasta bake in a golden covering of sauce in this Italian classic. Pre-cooked cannelloni tubes may be used but the dish must be baked and served right away or the shapes may burst. With conventional pasta, the dish may be assembled in advance and baked later.

8oz/225g lean minced beef
4oz/110g sausage meat
2 cloves garlic, finely chopped
6oz/170g/approx. ³/₄ cup ricotta or cream cheese
1 small egg
breadcrumbs
salt, pepper
12 cannelloni tubes
sauce napoli *(p.7)*
béchamel *sauce (p.4)*
freshly-grated Parmesan cheese

Fry the minced beef, sausage meat and garlic together until meat is lightly browned. Drain off fat and combine meat with the ricotta (or cream cheese) and egg. Mix in enough breadcrumbs to make manageable stuffing. Correct seasoning with salt and pepper. Cook cannelloni according to directions, until slightly underdone. Fill tubes with stuffing mixture and lay in a greased ovenproof dish. Pour Sauce Napoli evenly over cannelloni, then top with layer of *béchamel* and sprinkle with Parmesan cheese. Bake in oven pre-heated to gas mark 4, 350°F, 180°C until golden brown and bubbling, about 45 minutes.

Pasta Shells with Blue Cheese and Walnuts

Any sort of pasta can be used in this recipe, but shell shapes hold more of the delicious creamy sauce. Gorgonzola, Stilton, Danish Blue or Roquefort are just some of the many cheeses that are suitable.

10oz/280g medium pasta shells
6–8 tbsp/90–120ml/^{1}/$_3$–^{1}/$_2$ cup cream
5oz/145g blue cheese, crumbled
4 tbsp/60ml grated Parmesan cheese
freshly-ground black pepper
3oz/80g/^{3}/$_4$ cup walnuts, coarsely chopped

While pasta shells are cooking, heat cream with blue cheese and Parmesan cheese, blending until smooth. Season with black pepper, add walnuts and pour over hot cooked pasta to cover.

Rigatoni with Olive and Tuna Sauce

Tuna and tomatoes team up to make a quick main course pasta perfect for busy day meals or unexpected visitors.

14oz/400g rigatoni
2 tbsp/30ml olive oil
1 clove garlic, crushed
2 large tomatoes, peeled and chopped
1 tbsp/15ml tomato purée
25 stuffed green olives
6¹/₂oz/185g tin of tuna, well drained
freshly-ground black pepper

While rigatoni is cooking, combine olive oil, tomatoes, garlic, tomato purée and olives in a blender and process briefly. Heat sauce with flaked tuna, season with black pepper and pour over hot pasta.

Chicken Tetrazzini

Despite the Italian-sounding name, this dish appears to have originated in America. It is a good buffet dish, amenable to being made in quantity for entertaining.

10oz/280g spaghetti
1oz/25g/2 tbsp butter
8oz/225g mushrooms, sliced
2 stalks celery, thinly sliced
5 spring onions, chopped
1oz/25g/4 tbsp flour
8 fl oz/225ml/1 cup chicken stock
8 fl oz/225ml/1 cup cream
1¹/₄ lb/575g/3 cups cooked chicken meat, diced
freshly-grated Parmesan cheese
1oz/25g/¹/₄ cup slivered almonds

Cook spaghetti *al dente*. Melt butter and sauté mushrooms, celery and onions until softened. Stir in flour and add chicken stock. Continue stirring until liquid is smooth and slightly thickened. Add cream and allow to thicken before stirring in chicken. Combine chicken and sauce with cooked spaghetti and transfer to greased ovenproof dish. Top with grated Parmesan cheese and slivered almonds and bake in oven pre-heated to gas mark 5, 375°F, 190°C for about 30 minutes.

Seafood Pasta Bake

Mixed colours of pasta shapes or noodles can look very well in this delectable seafood main course. The relative amounts of white fish and more expensive prawns can be adjusted according to the occasion and the state of the budget. Serve with a crisp salad and crusty bread.

4oz/110g/1 cup cooked smoked haddock, flaked
4oz/110g/1 cup cooked white fish, flaked
4oz/110g/1 cup shelled cooked mussels
4oz/110g/1 cup shelled cooked prawns or shrimps
2 tsp chopped fresh dill or 1 tsp dried
1/2 pt/280ml/1 1/3 cups prepared béchamel sauce
salt, black pepper
2–3 tsp lemon juice
12oz/340g/approx. 3 1/2 cups cooked pasta
4 tbsp/60ml buttered breadcrumbs

Check cooked fish for bones and skin, then combine with mussels and prawns, dill and *béchamel* sauce. Season to taste with salt, pepper and lemon juice. Stir cooked pasta into seafood mixture and turn into well-greased ovenproof dish; top with breadcrumbs. Bake in oven pre-heated to gas mark 5, 375°F, 190°C until bubbling hot and golden brown on top, about 25 minutes.

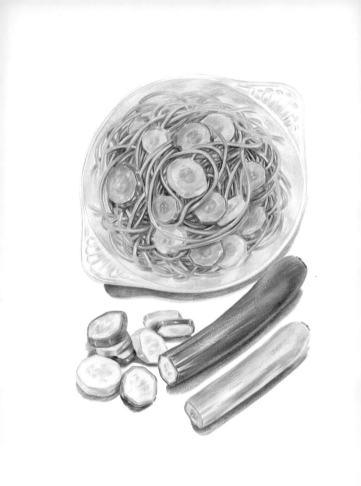

Spaghetti con Zucchini

The goodness of simple things is highlighted in this simple dish from the south of Italy. It looks especially inviting when made with a mixture of yellow and green courgettes. A simple dish like this deserves the very best fresh Parmesan cheese, hand grated just before using.

1 lb/450g small courgettes
salt
14oz/400g spaghetti
1¹/₂ tbsp/22g butter
1¹/₂ tbsp/22g olive oil
freshly-ground black pepper
fresh Parmesan cheese

Wash and slice courgettes, sprinkle with salt and place in a colander to drain for about 45 minutes. When ready, rinse courgettes in cold water, drain, and press dry in a tea towel. Put spaghetti to cook in salted boiling water. Heat butter and olive oil together in a pan and gently cook courgettes until soft. Drain cooked spaghetti and toss in cooked courgettes. Season well with black pepper and serve with freshly grated Parmesan cheese.

Smoked Salmon and Pasta Salad

Elegant *roulades* of smoked salmon top pale green pasta salads for an unusual dinner-party starter. Like the other best-behaved dishes for entertaining, it is mostly done in advance and assembled just before serving.

¹/₄ pt/140ml/²/₃ cup whipping cream
3 tbsp/45ml horseradish sauce
1 tbsp/15ml parsley, finely chopped
1 tbsp/15ml snipped chives
salt, pepper
8oz/225g smoked salmon, thinly sliced
8oz/225g green tagliatelle or fettucine
olive oil
mixed green salad leaves
(mache, rocket, endive, chicory, etc.)
lemon juice

Whip cream until very stiff, then fold in horseradish sauce, parsley and chives. Season with salt and pepper. On a large piece of foil or greaseproof paper, lay out slices of smoked salmon, overlapping pieces as necessary to form several rectangles. Spread the creamed mixture over the smoked salmon in an even layer and roll up carefully. Wrap rolls in cling film or foil and place in refrigerator to chill. Cook tagliatelle, drain and toss in a little olive oil to prevent sticking. Leave to cool. Arrange salad leaves on individual serving plates and make a nest of tagliatelle in the centre. With a sharp knife, cut the chilled smoked salmon rolls into slices and place several pieces on top of each pasta salad. Just before serving, dress salads with a little olive oil and lemon juice.

Green Bean and Pasta de Luxe

Swiss cheese, pasta and creamy sauce dress up green beans for serving as a vegetarian main course or along with plain grilled steaks or chops. Summer savoury is the classic bean herb, and it is sold dried if fresh savoury isn't available.

8oz/225g pasta bows, shells or other shapes
8oz/225g thin green beans
1oz/25g/2 tbsp butter
2 tbsp/30ml onion, very finely chopped
2 tbsp/30ml flour
6 fl oz/170ml/³/₄ cup commercial sour cream
1 tsp fresh chopped summer savoury (¹/₂ tsp dried)
salt, pepper
4oz/110g Swiss Emmenthal cheese, shredded

Cook pasta until just *al dente*. Blanch green beans in boiling salted water 3–5 minutes, so they are cooked but still crisp; drain and set aside. Melt butter over gentle heat and cook onion until soft. Stir in flour, cook for a minute, then stir in sour cream. Season with summer savoury, salt and pepper, and cook briefly without allowing to boil. Combine sauce with cooked green beans and pasta and turn into greased flameproof dish. Top with Swiss cheese and grill until cheese melts and starts to colour. Serve immediately.

Coronation Pasta Salad

Delicate curry and chutney seasonings make an appealing main course for summer. It is easy and economical to make in quantity for buffet entertaining.

2 tbsp/30ml dry sherry
8oz/225g/about 2 cups cooked chicken, diced
6 fl oz/170ml/³/₄ cup good mayonnaise
4 spring onions, finely chopped
1 tsp tomato purée
1 tsp lemon juice
¹/₂ tsp curry powder
2 tbsp/30ml apricot chutney
salt
8oz/225g/about 3 cups cooked pasta shapes
chicory leaves
toasted flaked almonds

Sprinkle sherry over cooked chicken and set aside. Combine mayonnaise with onions, tomato purée, lemon juice, curry powder and chutney. Taste and salt if necessary. Stir together the sherried chicken, sauce and pasta. Arrange chicory leaves in a circle on a large platter, spoon salad mixture into centre and sprinkle with toasted almonds.

Chinese Beef and Noodle Stir-Fry

Chinese egg noodles are the ones sold in sheets like bits of ravelly knitting. They are generally merely steeped or only briefly cooked in boiling water. As in all stir-frying, the success of this dish depends on quick cooking over fierce heat.

12oz/340g topside or rump steak
1 clove garlic, crushed
1 tbsp/15ml soy sauce
1 tbsp/15ml brown sugar
1 tbsp dry sherry
6oz/170g Chinese egg noodles
peanut oil
6 spring onions, sliced
1 sweet red pepper, cut into strips
sesame oil

Semi-freeze beef, then slice into paper thin strips. Make marinade of garlic, soy sauce, sugar and sherry, stir into sliced beef and leave for ¹/₂ an hour. Cook egg noodles according to directions and drain. Heat peanut oil in wok or deep-frying pan and quickly stir-fry the beef, which has been drained of marinade. Put beef aside and stir-fry noodles for a few minutes, then add spring onions and pepper strips. Return beef to wok with other ingredients and cook all together for a minute. Sprinkle with sesame oil and serve immediately.

Pasta Cheese Ring

This baked pasta shape is designed to hold your choice of fresh-cooked vegetables in a cream sauce, or simply buttered and seasoned. Mushrooms, baby spring vegetables or brussel sprouts in cheese sauce are a few successful options.

8oz/225g green or white tagliatelle
2 eggs, separated
4 fl oz/110ml/^{1}/$_2$ cup milk
1 tbsp/15ml butter, melted
2oz/50g/^{1}/$_2$ cup grated mature cheddar
pinch of salt
a little grated nutmeg

Cook tagliatelle and drain well. Beat together the egg yolks, milk, melted butter, cheese, salt and nutmeg. Combine with the cooked pasta. Beat the egg whites until stiff but not dry and fold into pasta mixture. Spoon into a well-greased 7 in / 18 cm ring mould. Set mould into a shallow pan of hot water and bake at gas mark 4, 350°F, 180°C until set, about 35 minutes. Turn out onto hot dish and serve filled with creamed vegetables.

Pasta Piedmontese

A quick and flavoursome sauce for this garlic-lovers' treat has its origins in *bagna cauda*, the "hot bath" dipping sauce from Piedmont in Italy.

3oz/75g/good handful of fresh green beans
1/2 cauliflower, broken into small florets
2 large carrots, cut into thin matchsticks
2oz/50g/4 tbsp butter
3 cloves garlic, crushed
8 anchovy fillets, drained
5 tbsp/75ml olive oil
12 oz/350g tagliatelle

Break the topped and tailed green beans into bite-size lengths and cook in boiling salted water with cauliflower and carrot sticks for 4–5 minutes, or until just lightly cooked. Drain and put aside. To make sauce, melt butter in a pan with garlic and cook gently for a minute. Add anchovies and mash to help them disintegrate. Add olive oil and keep hot while tagliatelle is cooking in boiling salted water. When pasta is cooked, stir prepared vegetables into hot sauce and pour over drained tagliatelle.

Index